daily basis

# daily basis

poems by

# robert lovitt

*first thought press*
olympia, washington

Copyright © 2004 by Robert Lovitt
all rights reserved
For information or additional copies,
write: *First Thought Press* 3029 46th Ave. NE, Olympia, WA 98506
email: dailybasis@comcast.net

Cover Design by Paul Tompkins (www.tallpumpkins.com)

Library of Congress Control Number: 2004092766
ISBN: 0-9753881-0-X

First Edition

Published by *First Thought Press*
Printed by Gorham Printing 2004

Dedicated to Allen Ginsberg (who cut through), Chogyam Trungpa (who threw open the vault), Patricia Donegan (who handed out the 17 syllables), Milarepa (who defined exertion), Osel Tenzin (who kept my tie), Lawrence Ferlinghetti (who walked a tightrope to get to the other side), Steve Marsh (relentless editor/comrade extraordinaire), Harvey Stein (navigator of the Pen ship), Murray Gordon (the beat who goes on), Judy Robison (who listens), Barbara Gibson (for big-sistering me), everyone else on the bus, and sweetfriend companion Elizabeth Fischer (who remains- somehow- nearby)…

## acknowledgments

many of these poems, in various versions, first appeared in the following publications, to which grateful acknowledgement is made:

*atom mind* – laundromat - montréal snowing
*beacon review* – lake washington
*black bough* – narrow tracks to the amtrak south
*brussles sprouts* – admiring the straight sapling
*the christian science monitor* – my norman rockwell poem, through the rust
*dragonfly* – green-eyed cat
*frogpond* – summer snapshots
*haiku zasshi zo* – she left her address, the crow swoops, admiring the straight sapling, outside and leaning, footsteps
*jam to-day* – her shadow undresses
*jewish frontier* – friday afternoon, it didn't matter, sender zahler
*jewish spectator* – still swinging
*moody street irregulars* – one sprig of hyacinth
*open sky studio* – sender zahler
*the phoenix* – downtown
*the plaza* (japan) – red berries, the tomatoes don't ripen
*redoubt* (australia) – listening for her footsteps
*silver trumpet* – like a child curled, camping on the moon
*skyviews* – listening for her footsteps
*smoke signals* – mobile american poet

**contents**

*autumn*

the tomatoes don't ripen  (10)
my wife's health horoscope  (11)
teacher heaven  (12)
outside and leaning  (13)
through the rust  (14)
footsteps  (15)
kisses  (16)

*winter*

my norman rockwell poem  (18)
beyond the clouds  (19)
there are no demons  (20)
laundromat - montréal snowing  (21)
friday afternoon/the jewish tailor's shop/rue laurier  (23)
it didn't matter  (24)
bows to earth  (25)
three chinese english teachers/after dinner poems - *sunset*  (26)
changing light  (27)

*spring*

one sprig of hyacinth  (29)
red berries  (30)
garlic grass and fallen plum blossoms  (31)
weight  (32)
upright buddha  (33)

*summer*

lake washington  (35)
answering machine  (36)
the moth flies away  (37)
julie burns  (38)
camping on the moon  (39)
eleven pelicans  (40)
narrow tracks to the amtrak south  (41)
downtown  (44)
le soleil est encore chaud  (45)

*sticks and stones and...*

smoke from the candles  (47)
like a child curled  (48)
final truce  (49)
hunter/gatherer  (50)
forget the chickens  (51)
sender zahler  (52)
still swinging  (54)
mobile american poet  (56)
ping-pong through the ages: a male perspective  (57)
only father guru  (60)
health club  (61)
close call  (62)
he watched two finches  (63)
infiltrating ductile carcinoma  (64)
she always was intelligent  (66)

*china/japan*

river viewing  (70)
golden summit temple, mt.emei  (71)
china snapshots  (72)
night streets in leshan  (74)
the poverty of poverty  (75)
japan snapshots  (76)
cuckoo's cry  (80)

moonlit

scarecrow

waves

his

white

gloved

hand -

the wind

i

guess

**autumn**

## the tomatoes don't ripen

each year it's the same thing
the tomatoes don't ripen
before the first rains

i have to pluck them
still green
from their wasting vines

they resist
holding on
like the hopes
of summer

but the sun is gone
surely gone

and i pickle them
in jars of vinegar and spices-

after a week
they taste full
sharp and lasting

i let the rains arrive
and eat them
cold
one by one

october 3, 1990 / seattle

## my wife's health horoscope
## predicts autumnal arthritis, suggests consulting a physician

i love your open hands
fingers swollen or no
in blue air
autumn
i will burnish
them with liniments
of pumpkin and apple
the working out
of touch-
to release the directions
of their random grasp
you'll find my warm skin
applicable
we'll weather the weather
become seasoned
by the season
there will be pain
we'll consult
the prominent planets
and soak fingers
in moonlight-
your hands will remain
open
beyond the twist
of clouds

september 21, 1992 / seattle

## teacher heaven

barefoot in my office at 5:20 pm
charlie hayden and pat metheny
*beyond the missouri sky*
on the
mellow jazz tape player –
guitar and bass

no sun setting sunset
worlds turn
beyond the continuous rain

my chinese students
down the hall
bent at small desks
studying my vocabulary words
as if they were important

me in this quiet office
bent at my wooden desk
symbiotic
correcting their papers
as if i was important

who can say this is not heaven?

february 7, 2000 / olympia

## outside and leaning

my lover
crying
again
outside
i lean
against
our
apartment
door -
more
rain

april 27, 1988 / seattle

# through the rust

night's prompt shadow
covers

without exception
even the mountains

their shoulders frozen
to the horizon

the lake wrinkles
to catch the stars

to bend and multiply
the moon's silver

near the houses
an occasional dog

strays from the halos
of street lamps

ferreting
all nose and tail

through the rust of
fallen leaves

october 16, 1982 / seattle

listening

for

her

footsteps

morning

comes

to

my

bed -

instead

february 12, 1986 / karme-choling, vt

## kisses

packed parking lot
overflowing
cars diving for streets curbs

in the waning light
hundreds arrive
for this funeral, this farewell

standing room only
and more outside in the cooling air
and the hallway

while inside
in the neatly-rowed church
all listen to the microphoned words

a father like robert frost
a sister like a shaking tree
a husband like a mountain

a daughter like a benediction
then the friends -
testimony heaped upon testimony

story after story
punctuated by song, by violin
by tears

a little girl, perhaps age four
wanders away from the hub of unpleasant drama
to the exit

where she kisses and kisses again
her own ghost-like reflection
in the church's glass door

september 7, 2000 / seattle

a

crow

swoops

down

to

stand

on

its

shadow

in

the

snow

winter

## my norman rockwell poem

the newspaper boy
with a saddle
of newspapers
over his shoulder
and orange safety
reflector tape
on his glasses-frame
just walked by my window
with another boy
an apprentice
who with frozenbreath
followed behind-
learning the porches
learning the dogs

december 23, 1983 / seattle

# beyond the clouds

the gray sky
blue behind the clouds
the computer screen empty behind the words

geese in loose v formation
point their long-necks
towards somewhere and wing over our house

in the garden
lemon crocuses
already in bloom despite our winter calendar

miniature purple irises
delicately open
encircling the golden buddha statue

from the other room
the tv blares
war ships converging in persian gulf déjà vu

our neighbor's
dustbrown rooster
salutes the sun

between cracks of cloud


january 18, 1991 / seattle

 there are no demons

there are no demons
        just a long braid
                of jet black twisted hair
                        obscene/sensual
silver spiked medieval
        through and into this
                askew front door
                      twisting in
  the numbing night wind
        that swaggles through
                what was once called
                      our town
at the wind's discretion
        it brushes or muffledly knocks
                a spongy sound
                      that only some can hear
a door is so
        unlike the sweep
                of a fervid
                      neck
there are no demons
        just demon memorabilia
                a photograph from 1979
                      and a few of her penned letters
there are no demons
        just john coltrane
                set to play and replay
                      *invitation*
                              to the ethereal winter night

january 3, 2003 / olympia

# laundromat - montréal snowing

across the street - a barbecue shop
four-tiered spit turning fat chickens

open from 8 a.m. to midnight
could you eat a chicken at 8 a.m.?

fruit store window
- a crumbling pyramid
green apples - 59¢

green stripes on a white awning
and a kid walking by
with a kickball

which he tosses up onto it
the ball twirling
and rolling back down

fast off the curved canvas -
i'm all alone
in the laundromat

even the chinese girl
with bad acne has left
they all come in,

pop clothes into a machine
and leave
back only to heave wet clothes

into dryers
always right on time
or close

where the hell do they go
in between?
home to dirty a quick towel?

i however, persevere
- *laundry purist*
waiting patiently

for my machine to finish
my jeans not really damp
enough to justify

another 25 cent dry,
but it's so comfortable here
looking out the window

to watch a kid pee in the alley
or down at my book
- to write this in the margin

december 22, 1981 / montréal

friday afternoon
the jewish tailor's shop/rue laurier




i stepped into the usual clutter
unclaimed pants  phone numbers  brown forgotten plants
yiddish books on the counter
feeble overhead lights dusting the beige walls
      the stooped tailor (who had teased me because
      my jeans all wore thin in the crotch) wasn't there
*"abe's got a cold"*  his wife explained
      contemplating the broken zipper on my winter coat
her voice incredulous repeating my request
      *"you vant i should fix it right now?"*
that she should drop more important piece work
to mend my coat then snatching it from my arms
as if it were a baby held by a man
who couldn't hush its crying
      from the ancient sewing machine
          berating me for having to change the color of the thread
          her foot on the pedal
          scowling at the coat which wasn't worth her time
yet walking up to me a few minutes later
smiling and saying i could have it for free
laughing and adding - *"or for the price of a coffee"*
      while i fumbled with my wallet
      insisting she at least take the dollar bill i held out
her taking it and breaking the embarrassed silence
      shooing me
*"so go already - time is money - i have more important
things to do than to talk to you all day"*
      she headed back to her waiting machine
      adding in an entirely different voice:
*"good shabbos"*
      as i turned
      and stepped back outside
      onto the sidewalk - filling with snow


february 12, 1982 / montréal

## it didn't matter

it didn't matter that outside it was trying to snow
while we sat over coffee and bagels

me with a quaker in a jewish deli
her bleak smiles

it didn't make a difference
that our waitress was asian

or that the suited men behind us
were discussing insurance or car oil

and it mattered not that the old women
behind her were bent like birds over seed

wearing sweaters they had no intention
of ever taking off

and who cares how mediocre the omelet was
or that the orange juice was too expensive to order

all i knew was that on the next day i'd be gone
and that her hand would be further away

much further than the distance
across that table-top sheen

march 10, 1981 / cincinnati

 **bows to earth**

storm

broken

birch

formerly

of heaven

bows

now

to

earth

january 7, 1986 / karme-choling, vt

## three chinese english teachers - after dinner poems - *sunset*

much unsaid
        *sunset glitters on the beads*
and many shining words
        *of the curtains. spring flowers*
liang li hua and hu dan
        *bloom in the valley. the gardens*
soar like qi gong cranes
        *along the river are filled*
with elizabeth, my wife
        *with perfume. smoke of cooking*
in the wood heated living room
        *fires drifts over the slow barges.*
while i share with jiang tao
        *sparrows hop and tumble in*
this english translation
        *the branches. whirling insects*
of tu fu- which he reads aloud, words
        *swarm in the air. who discovered*
between sips of wine-
        *that one cup of thick wine*
this timeless tongue
        *will dispel a thousand cares?*

february, 26, 2000 / olympia

# changing light

three extraordinarily beautiful
coyotes in the laundromat's
sun lighted window

so dazzling in the light
creasing their striped towels
near piles of folded sheets

but fickle, the sun suddenly
hides behind the clouds and one
fills a green plastic garbage bag

with her clothes and then departs
one coyote remains at the folding
table dreamily applying red/brown polish

to long fingernails as
the other stares out the darkened window
catching my eye

and smiling sadly

february 15, 1982 / montréal

admiring

the

straight

sapling

an

old

man

leans

on

his

shovel

**spring**

# one sprig of hyacinth

the entire

north american

continent

kept its blended

whiskey in a

jigger glass

on the

white oak

shelf above

her bed

where she

had one sprig

of hyacinth

leaning out

of an empty

frozen

orange juice

can

march 28, 1982 / seattle

petals flee the magnolia tree riding slants of rain-
moss paved green sidewalk where lichens cover the stack
of winter soaked logs

already the crocuses, already the wild onions-
just spring and a bumblebee bee-seated
on a garbage can lid

pale blue border, forget-me-nots, path the winding hill to the lake
down to weeping willows bent in sad watch of sailboats
that lean the horizon

coatblown kids turn the beach upside-down
with kick balls and shouts
sea gulls terrace the clouds, the juniper wears

red berries

april 21, 1983 / seattle

## garlic grass and fallen plum blossoms

full grown light brownishgray rabbit
fleeing from the old cat
scrambling, escaping

        but scurrying so fast he can't see
        the faint olive colored wires

and he gets himself snared in the backyard fence
jammed there three quarters of the way through
his hind legs and back end stuck

        garlic grass and fallen plum blossoms
        mix with the damp scent of fear

every muscle straining forward
making flesh cut and fur stain red
eyes bulging, the unhurried cold of night closing in

        eventually out of strength, he surrenders
        under the pinpoints of soundless stars

the morning sun
finds him caught in place
caught lifeless

and altogether free

may 2, 1997 / olympia

weight

the

weight

of

gliding

moonlight

on

the

plum tree -

one

blossom

falls

april 17, 1997 / olympia

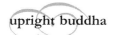
# upright buddha

upright buddha, pearly porcelain
so like a statue
he is a statue

silent eyes closed
listening to the twilling
of rufous pileated somethings

listening as pickup trucks
brake for the stop sign

listening to arias of the air
the dakinis' operettas of universal wisdom
or maybe they are just crows
cawing a contingency plan of sanity

the upright buddha
hears the overhead roar
of air force cargo planes

flying west to go east
ladling materials from
the tranquil isle of northwest
splashing them into the boundless ocean of war
then returning for more and more

the buddha is surrounded
encircled by leaning daffodils
that vibrate their yellowness

upright buddha
surrounded by the morning chill
the chattering swallows -

my upright buddha
without thinking, without hesitation-
declares unconditional surrender

april 3, 2003/ olympia

full

moon

shadows

long

on

grassy

meadow-

shivering

**summer**

# lake washington

there are many other
dogs here also

some of them
tricked into the freezing lake

by sunday strolling masters
with weird chewed frisbees

unmerciful with
"go fetches" and "atta boys!"

i'm jogging
sweating, detached

from human mind
mangy and sure-footed

through the green duck shit
at the lake's edge

in a moment of heartbeatingconfusion
i spring at an unwinged arc

of toothy frisbee
cutting the sky

gulping my heart
good doggie! good doggie!

naw- i remain biped
and upright

bending up the hill
in removable clothing


december 21, 1982 / seattle

## answering machine

full moon
night quiet
blue house

we can do it

we did it before
if it has metastasized
we can deal with it

her doctor's voice
on the answering machine -
x-rays look good

full moon floats
over our blue house
buoyant in a sea of sky

june 7, 2000 / olympia

## the moth flies away

green-eyed

cat

*leaps*

into

the

wild onions

the

moth

flies

away

july 12, 1987 / seattle

julie burns
your name

is ink-black printed
towards the bottom

of my white bed-sheet
and ironed-on

near the label
at the top left seam with

little red block letters
on a white patch of cloth tape

no one could mistake your sheet
no one could take your sheet

i found it in a cardboard box
i had sitting for years

in a basement, in cincinnati
here in lonely colorado

julie burns, i sleep
on your summer night sheet

june 27, 1980 / boulder

## camping on the moon

camping on the moon is no easy thing
though it's true that the backpack is lighter
and tent stakes easier to pound home
into gray powdery indifference of moondirt
still there are difficulties

while one could bear the weight and enjoy the luxury of
bringing along canned goods
(soft sliced peaches in a light syrup for instance)
it's difficult, while suited up, to use a conventional can-opener
(the gloves have so little give)

but at night - to watch the earthrise -yes!
while snuggling next to your suited honey
his or her voice crackling in helmeted ear receiver
no atmosphere, just a thin visor between you and other worlds -
the infinite flitter of planets, stars

a romantic scene in black and white to be sure
but slipping together (or even alone) into any sleeping bag
while wearing a moon suit with a pack of oxygen
is cumbersome at best
especially with those shoes,

but the quiet is so startling, and the view so great
no matter what the travel costs, once there, it feels worth the effort
and when it is time, going home will surely be a drag -
back to the full weight of earth-bound life
back to the primary colors and airy bustle

october 9, 1992 / seattle

## eleven pelicans

eleven pelicans, one after the other
on invisible skytracks

eleven pelicans wing indiscriminately
over beautiful beach house roofs/and ugly concrete condos

eleven pelicans
suspended unmoving/in florida ringing bluesky

eleven pelicans
float over the shifting dunes/heading for the shifting sea

eleven pelicans
eleven pelican shadows/weave the white beach

august 7, 1997 / st. augustine

# narrow tracks to the amtrak south

## *washington*

"all aboard" unyelled
i climb onto the train/anyway

for choice seats
and overhead luggage space/we scramble-shamelessly

not out of the station
looking forward/to coming home

two japanese girls
play cards/cozy- in stocking feet

sloshed in the lounge car
salesmen compare the size/of their territory

abandoned car
roof caved-in/farmer in an expanse of greens

the train curves
i count the snaking cars/eight

conductor down the aisle
really does say/"tickets, tickets please"

old rv park
rusted empty drums/blackberries

first tunnel-kids thrilled
adults see their own reflections/in the black windows

staggering down the aisle
in red plaid pants/an old man-lost

abandoned drive-in
screen curled/speaker poles in the high grass

cows and sexy billboard faces
watch us wind past/without expression

*oregon*

pink woman
picking up the newspaper/slowly in her wrinkled robe

freight doors
the backs of portland warehouses/bleak afternoon

at crossings- sweet pleasure
being in the train/cars stop for me

reading the bible
middle-aged woman next to me/sips her beer

yellow purple white
fields of brown irises/long after blooming

giving us the "finger"
with both hands/farm boy from his safe porch

field of cabbage
field of tombstones

two black girls
lead the drunken white woman/back to her seat

church parking lot
woman in blue blouse/waving to us

a lake
lone fishing boat/just before sunset

snow peaked mountain
not wondering/what it's named

clickety-clack
a metal lullaby/amtrak cradle

## *california*

first light
davis california/palm trees!

squirming all night
at 6:30 a.m./i hate anyone who slept well

dining car luxury
eggs over easy/brown california hills

hispanic kid
garden hose between his legs/pretending to pee

trailer parks
subdivisions/the car steward has sleepy dark eyes

laundry like a butterfly collection
pinned stiff in place/no wind

the train brakes and slows
pulling me away/from a dream

one black man
carrying a paper bag-alone/on the train platform

oakland-a bent man
pulls a cart up/unloads our bags-of garbage

climbing off the train
bright sun/the unswaying world

august 17, 1990 / seattle – san francisco

# downtown

the moon is full
as a dime

propped in the black sky
by that enormous crane

the night is cool
the last of summer

a man staggers
towards the bus

and shouts
at those who wait

with their grocery bags
and worries:

"look at the wind
it's beautiful!! look!!

look at the wind!!"
a poet or a fool

the trees tremble
in their cemented feet

the metal crane
releases the moon

and it floats
away

september 4, 1983 / seattle

## le soleil est encore chaud

| | |
|---|---|
| the sun is still hot | le soleil est encore chaud |
| but the wind is fresh | mais le vent est frais |
| it penetrates | il pénètre |
| all the apple trees | tous les pommiers |
|    the trees are rich |    les arbres sont riches |
|    with their heavy jewels |    avec leurs bijoux lourds |
|    of red/green |    de rouge/vert |
| the sun starts to set | le soleil commence a se couche |
| as usual | comme d'habitude |
| in fact | au fait |
| everything is as usual | tout est comme d'habitude |
| but suddenly | mais tout à coup |
| one thinks | on pense |
| that maybe this is the last | que peut-être c'est le dernier |
| the last sun of summer | le dernier soleil de l'été |
|    in the dovecot |    dans le dovecot |
|    there are no pigeons |    il n y pas des pigeons |
|    they have departed |    ils sont partis |
|    during one century |    pendant un siècle |
|    or another |    ou un autre |
|    for some reason |    pour quelque raison |
|    or for another |    ou pour une autre |
| the wind becomes stronger still | le vent devient le plus fort |
| one can hear | on peut entendre |
| an owl | un hibou |
| he is early | il est tôt |
| in advance of the dark night | avant la nuit sombre |
|    and he announces |    et il annonce |
|    to no one particular |    à personne en particulier |
| in a voice exact | dans une voix exacte |
| and decisive | et décisif |
|    "the summer is gone" |    « l'été est parti » |

september 3, 2003 equemauville, france

she

left

her

address —

small

white

paper

sitting

inside

my shoe

**sticks
and stones
and…**

# smoke from the candles

many of my closest manfriends
these days

throw their own birthday parties
like our moms did for us - when we were kids

for most i buy at least
2 boxes of little candles

or being adults sometimes
we just use a symbolic number

today the birthday boy
wishes for a lover - he's 46

the smoke from his blown-out candles
sets off the smoke detector alarm

we get together for birthdays
like when we were boykids

the wishes are slightly more complex
less expected to come true

october 31, 1991 / seattle

# like a child curled

my alarm sounds
desperate
it's another day

my lover sleeps - like a child curled
without worry
without the beating affairs of money

she turns towards the wall
my dreams hide themselves
i kiss her tumbling hair

my feet touch the beige carpet
my clothes rest
on top of the chest

and on the floor
clothing of candid work
the room is dark, quiet

my breath arrives and departs
it is good
the day is fresh and undeniable

january 20, 1988 / seattle

# final truce

after our fight
i mop the kitchen/with anger and comet cleanser

unchanged
over the same things/arguing in the same way

sometime i'll try that
driving away/you look so dramatic

sitting alone
the sunny backyard/clouded with rage

wind slams
the screen door, not you/i wait some more

your car returns
engine shuts/silence

offering peace plans
on the front steps/before you'll enter

in the movie house
you whisper - "i love you"/a final truce


october 13, 1991 / seattle

 **hunter/gatherer**

at midnight
she goes out

with a knife
and flashlight

to cut
the irises

their blossoms bent
with falling snow

this morning
on the breakfast table

a yellow bouquet

march 5, 1991 / seattle

**forget the chickens** (after w.c.w.)

so much depends

upon

a woman in green

sweater

hands in pants pocket

leaning

against the white

pillar

october 19, 1982 / boulder

sender zahler

sender zahler folds and saves scraps of paper, napkins, rubber bands
and offers them to me - calling them "gelt"
sender lives in jewish general hospital
the tag on the back of his robe reads: "i belong to 4 northwest"
sender whistles the song "three blind mice"
and tells me it's an opera by wagner

after the war sender came to montréal from austria
and worked for years as a jeweler designing in gold and precious stone
sender is a jew, his god, however wasn't there to break the fall
when he smacked his head on the bathroom floor
sender now sees threads in the air - sender is not the man he used to be

sender shows me messages on kleenex, sees the ocean on the tiled floor
and explains to me in german why he wants to leave
sender pees in hallway garbage cans, asks for white wine with his meal
he looks through *eaton's* christmas catalogue holding it upside down
counting the folds in a picture of drapes
suddenly throwing it to the floor and saying to me "come, let's go"
i trudge behind as he invades the nurses' station - looking for diamonds

sender thinks he's in a post office and complains about the slow service
or in a hotel and can't find the ballroom
sender says his roommate is 90% stupid - poor mr. ornstein
who spends an entire afternoon trying to turn over in bed
sender sees a heavy nurse bend over - nudges me with an elbow
and asks: "did you see? she has two and a half tushies!"

in the afternoons he paces on untiring legs
passing an old man getting off the elevator, here to visit someone
sender says to no one "that's the barber"
it turns out- yes- he was one of the barbers in dreaded auschwitz
the other place where 40 years ago sender endured imprisonment
sender looks for a taxi, for exits, up and down the halls for hours
he asks if i have a car to take him "to the other side"
or to a different hotel where we can relax and maybe catch a show

finally lulled by dinner and sedatives
he sits tied into a chair fiddling with his robe
mumbling a reply when the loudspeaker pages a doctor
yawning and waiting to be put to bed
sender rests his chin on his chest and drifts off

into the freedom of borderless sleep...

novermber 27, 1981 / montréal

## still swinging

my mom wrote me
that frank adams
(my best friend in third grade)
is now a lawyer, married
and living in miami beach

which is funny
because in my dreams
he and i are still
in the art room closet
supposedly straightening out
the supplies
of colored papers and paints

but actually hanging on shelf-posts
like the monkeys at the zoo
us stringing stories and jokes
together about everyone
and especially
about the art teacher
who we think is pregnant
though we don't really know
what that means

and all the while
tossing a sponge ball
back and forth
and through the shelves
with amazing accuracy
and we're three or four feet
above the floor floating
like inside a spaceship - weightless
no world outside

and the ball sooner or later
careening off a glue bottle
or something

and angle-ing kaboom!
right into a palm
no matter how busy we are
laughing and swinging and -

i hope frank likes miami


february, 1982 / seattle

## mobile american poet

i am the mobile american poet
electric typewriter mounted in the dash of my car
push a button and copies appear in the glove compartment

i type on cloverleaves, on turnpikes, under passes
at 60 miles per hour i make gas station attendants immortal
or put "howard johnson's" in stanzas

back seat filled with typing ribbons and blank sheets
the addresses of publishing companies on the back of my visor
i'm the mobile american poet, maybe you'll see me around

i stop for fuel at a. & w. root beer stands
my thumb on a texaco map, mobile american poet
typing and driving into the night

i sting routes together like adjectives, my commas are rest areas
if i lived anywhere, i'd be home by now
i'm the mobile american poet, fingers flying as tires spin

i see the country through a windshield, my engine and typewriter
blending into the sound of america - my exhaust salutes the world!
mobile american poet, driving ideas into the ground

my car rides high on roads and words
my bumper says: "don't follow me, i'm lost too"
i'm the mobile american poet - and i drive alone

july 5, 1980 / boulder

### ping-pong through the ages: a male perspective
(for my father who taught it, david who played it, and mike - who still plays)

ping-pong didn't exist before 1959
for me
till we went to florida - miami
and at the "baghdad" motel, pool side
50 yards away from the atlantic
sat an outdoor aqua green
all weather table
under the blazing sun!

human fathers have taught human sons
to read clouds for rain, where to forage
how to survive, when to plant
-my father taught me ping-pong

"put some english on it, undercut, and they'll net it"
"spin to the right and they'll return to the left"
in white t-shirt and baggy swim trunks
his paddle would butterfly the ocean breeze
here he was king, he was mentor
each instruction i'd imprint
-winning another game
he'd dismiss his pupil for the day
always leaving me with the advice:
"don't trifle with the master"
"never trifle with the master"

25 years before the term "male bonding" was coined,
in my parent's cincinnati basement
on a plywood board with improvised net
david levy and i would perform our art
this was our suburban cave
the smells not of ocean, but wet laundry and bug spray
our banter combined the wisdom of tv the numbers 1 through 21
the anatomy and mystery of girls we knew

and girls we didn't
our art demanded its own language
this is how we kept score:
at 1 to 1 you say "i wanna piece"
at 2 to 1 you say "doubled your score"
at 1 to 4 it was "one for the road"
at 7 to 7 you say "seven-up- that's my favorite drink!"
at 8 to 8 you say "ate a piece"
-the afternoons were suspended
like ceilings

in college, "pong" had a different impact
took on a different importance -at this point
ping-pong had evolved from the 50's and 60's
and had thickened with vague political implications
nixon had been to china
ping-pong was diplomacy, it was an oriental art
it was like mind training, like zen
distraction was an enemy
it was male, it was competitive
it was about confidence

during the past decades
the sweet sounds of pong receded
as i searched for meaning elsewhere
-occasionally seeking refuge from a boring party of talk
i'd find a cool basement
my shirt sleeves rolled

here in seattle, my neighbor is retired
has a table out near his garage
tonight, he was paddle in hand
looking for a game-
i went over and played - arms uncoiling
once again - a table
once again - the sounds of a metronome
gone mad
mind training - like zen
a cave of laundry

the smell of the ocean
my paddle a butterfly
like yours dad – like yours


july 25, 1989 / seattle

## only father guru

now that you have died
i am truly an orphan
and it is sad to live alone
in this world
sad to live alone
in this cement samsara
but through the foresight
of your limitless compassion
my inheritance is immeasurable
though my sight is veiled
by the darkness of ignorance, passion and aggression,
you have left the great eastern sun
to light my path
though my heart is cold and narrow
you have opened up your treasury
of limitless warmth
though my skills are meager
you have given me the 6 rungs of paramita
to cross over the turbulent river
of despairing-mind
though my knowledge is slight
you have left open the vaults
of true insight
there is no way to thank you
for these gifts
except to share this wealth
with *all* sentient beings
i vow in the direction
of the rigden kings - to do so
and in the tradition
of the practice lineage
and in your name
chogyam trungpa

april 5, 1987 / karme-choling, vt

health club

all you college boys, women paralegals
old men wearing gold fertility necklaces
    come in together, male and female
    enter the separate realms - locker rooms!
breathe these bodies, towels and hair tonics
in a rusty locker, leave work clothes on a hook
    slap your feet on the cold naked floor, lace your
    gym shoes, adjust your straps, check your weight
enter the bowels of health club!
celebrate these muscles moving metal
    curl forward, propel back, out of the cradle
    endlessly rowing, through l.c.d. readout time
watch the bicyclers hunch handlebars
flipping magazines, detached with walkman eyes
    leotard skin over skin, triangles
    of triangles, roundness of round
everything private is in public view!
all these bodies as yet undecayed!
    stretch in front of the mirrored wall, become a
    semaphore of muscled limb, spell firm! spell fit!
on the indoor track, unband your legs, let your
head float off, a balloon over your body jogging
    foot meeting floor, foot meeting floor, 'round and
    'round healthy, between birth and uninvited death
shower the locker room fantastic!
sing the body mechanical!
    wrap clothes over an unwrinkled body
    give off steam under the starry night
die not young, but ancient
feed forever - this body of light

february 7, 1990 / seattle

close call

in the middle
of the dining room mandala
we are standing on blue tiles near the wood stove
when unexpectedly
she extends her hand consciousness
towards my crown chakra
my eye consciousness
magnetized - her low cut beige blouse
her corporal heavings
rising and falling
heatedly into clarity
she is twiddling my hair consciousness
her throat chakra gurgles forth
a gentle fountain of word sounds
 "you are such a handsome man"
enter my ear consciousness
my ego solidity expands exponentially
but mind consciousness speedily
blushes conventional awareness to the skin surface
- o she is inebriated with the night
- o inebriated with distilled grains
- o we are standing too close
- o my wife is in the next room
- o the other guests are not frozen in time like we are

in the middle
of the dining room mandala
my throat consciousness clears itself
excuses and extricates itself
and its no-self
to go into the kitchen
to get some more
hors d'oeuvres

april 4, 2003 / olympia

# he watched two finches

he doesn't seem to be engaging
he's not convoying his habitual reinforcements:
briefcase, coffee thermos, tidy piles
towards the community college
and his awaiting students
and his pressing tasks

it's time to leave, but he is hesitating
his inner truant wants to call in sick
excuses preprinted in his mind:
laziness, spring

earlier that morning he watched
two finches chasing and shadowing each other
through the strain of chattering dawnlight
through the thick bushes that side their house

he wants his still-in-bed wife
to also call in sick

two grey finches
flitting between branches
between the azalea's crimson blossoms
warbling and finching and chasing
each other

he backs the car out of the garage
his wife now awake
at the living room window
waving goodbye to him -
waving and singing
her perfect morning song

may 2, 2003 / olympia

## infiltrating ductile carcinoma

tumor that is 2.5cm wide by 2.3 cm long
the world upside down - the inherited history:

> her mother's breast then her mother's bones
> early death she's been all alone
> her mother's mother gone there too
> is there nothing doctors can do?

generations of cells marching to the off beat
of their own dna gone astray drumming
who knows if triggered by her childhood river water
in innocent drinking glass, water which first coursed
through churning turbines of chlorinated industrial ohio
air full of potato chips
and ivory soap, prell shampoo, duncan hines- too

she's dreaming wrapped around a pine tree,
a wolf licking her wound
she's in any hospital sleeping
her hand covering her eyes from the room's unkind brightness
i can see swallows swirling and the sea gulls
one flew off with her breast, it's gone
her center of gravity has been changed - forever

> hard enough to leave your mother's breast
> harder yet to leave your own
> someone say you love me
> the walls they do groan

amazon of dahomey let loose the arrow
that can disperse this pain,
this hospital gown of pain
good cancer patient, visualizing strong white blood cells
breathing in white light, sipping green tea
though it's impossible in the naked shower

an unending cascade of sobs
let the faucet stay open
it connects to the main pipe under the house
to dobbs creek and out to puget sound

good and bad happy and sad
may all scars fade like the imprint of a bird in the sky

the petro-chemical industry sent no get well card
the guys that give you pollutants sell you chemo
give you radiation
then steal and grind your bones
our center of gravity - changed forever
amazon of dahomey - let loose the arrow
that can pierce corporate heart

today we went to farmer's market
and bought sun colored tulips
and bought good-for-you collard greens
the newspaper headline was about funding cuts
for environmental cleanup
and their other new agendas

so we sing to every one out of eight women
    who might lose a breast
so we sing to the american cancer societies
    who've incorrectly said they know best
know that we know
    and that we'll continually attest:

        that   mammography is not prevention
            and detection is not a cure

march 17, 1995 / olympia

## she always was intelligent

you've got to be prudent
when you write the woman
that you went out with on your first ever date
some 35 years ago
after having dreamt about her so vividly last night

you must be careful how you word your email
and keep an eye on its tone
after all
you don't want her to think that you are unhappy
or that you are trying to rekindle an old flame
if you are not
[and you are *sure* that you're not]
or even worse-
you don't want her to think that
you are soliciting for alumni funds or something like that

you find her name in the class directory
along with the blurb: married, living in indiana, two kids

such succinct summary

part of you wanted her to be single or lesbian
living somewhere like boston or berkeley
you really only had one date with her
to a freshman frolic dance
a double date in fact
with barry and karen
who were engaged in openly erotic
handholding
in the plymouth backseat
that 1968 spring night

you had connected with her in junior high
she seemed to know your mind
she wasn't what they would then call "pretty"
but she was what they would now call – "spunky"

after that dance
you bribed her locker mate
into letting you put
a box of toys, little people
stuffed into a decorated band-aid box
in her locker, to leave it waiting
in the patient metal darkness for her to find

little figurine toys of our small lives
and wasn't there? – yes, a kind of - well, love note,
i guess you'd call it
that you had written and rewritten
the previous night

-you had never made
that kind of offering to anyone

anyway in your dream she is walking in a park
in your home town
with a woman friend, they are also middle-aged now
and they are glad to see you after all of these years
not knock-down-howling-glad
but intelligently and properly glad

she always was intelligent

she invites you back to her house to catch up on
the archaeologically covered and uncovered decades
that somehow have elapsed

her utility room floor is covered with her kids' dirty jeans
"a robust family life" you think to yourself

her husband is at work
he sounds like a nice guy
"you two have a great deal in common" she comments
the conversation unfolds -
she knows a lot about wine,

you know only the feel of the bottle's weight against your palm
she is a kind of connoisseur of the everyday-living arts
in fact she knows much regarding a multitude of things
while over time, you seem to know
less and less of things

one thing you do know though
is that it is time to go
to awaken from this dream

then in the morning (an early spring morning
like today's, in fact exactly today's)
you decide that you want to write her

though you haven't written her or talked to her
or even thought about her
for so many years

and you wonder what exactly to say
to this intelligent stranger
with whom for a few brief weeks
in another era
you were willing to share your teenaged heart

you must be careful
you don't want her to think
that you are just another fundraiser
for the old alma mater
you don't want her to think that you are unhappy
or that you are trying to rekindle an old flame

no, you have to make her a new, unmistakable kind of offering
and leave it waiting in this metal darkness
for her, in her own time
(in her own indiana, married, two kids time)
leave it waiting
right here
for her - to find

may 24, 2003 / olympia

flying

somewhere

a crow's

wing

brushes

against

the red

maple leaves

china/
japan

river viewing

would-be-bodhisattva goes for an evening walk
along the *min* river, ducking under the ginkgo trees
his feet following sidewalks that curve towards the river wall

night settling, bats winging from under the bridge
to feast on fruitful insects
electric lights shimmer from the other shore

there is no moon no stars no sky
only this perpetual blanket
of polluted cloud

the guardian dragons departed a few decades ago
only a distant dog barks
fish weep in these toxic waters

across the river, a mountain sized buddha is sitting
a model of carved rock equanimity
after 1300 years, he is flood-lit tonight for the tourists

they are being overcharged for speedboat rides
over and back across the *min*, boarding from
a questionable plank off the floating karaoke bar

would-be-bodhisattva is far from home
even the great tu fu and li po
did not wander this far from their "former gardens"

the speedboats cut back and forth
through the frothy night
would-be-bodhisattva's heart is tied by a rope to this moonless sky

summer, 1996 / leshan sichuan, china

# golden summit temple, mt.emei

above the sea of clouds
foliage-covered peaks protrude
nirvana is right here
at "self sacrifice crag"
it's a simple jump over the low railings
to alight forever in heaven

only the old pilgrims
come here to worship the buddha
most are here to enjoy
the view from the temple
this beauty under heaven
the sheer precipices and overhanging rocks

chinese tourists
in full-length rented red army jackets
swarm the temple grounds
drinking tea to stay the cold
talking excitedly
carrying cameras to capture the rising sun

would-be-bodhisattva
why are you here?
tear streaked, cross-legged
facing west, towards tibet
sunlight now starting to blaze on
the great snow mountains of the roof of the world

in this morning chill, only the old pilgrims
worship the buddha
others here just to enjoy the view
the great snow mountains to the west
remain unmoved
their peaks aloft
in the splintering of another sunrise

summer, 1996 / sichuan, china

 china snapshots

sitting in the back of the truck
on a load of green watermelons
a woman and her toothless smile

on the artificial pond
of the exclusive hotel
real dragonflies

hurled from a 14th floor apartment
into the ancient *min* river
another bag of garbage

on the bridge
after the car's headlights fade
darkness embraces the embracing lovers

yellow flowers dangling from a
trellis of squash, flutter from
the breeze of our passing bus

young man peddling a bike through the rice paddy
his wife balanced on the handlebars
holding their baby

sunset - a farmer in his riverbank bank
and a fisherman nearby
bent in separate harvests

bicycle, two woven baskets
ducks peep out
alive this one last day

water buffalo - "wow that's a shot"
throw open the bus window
too late

woman in red high heels
pushes shut the karaoke club door
at 8:36 a.m.

along side our bus, a taxi
one watermelon
rolling in the empty back seat

in the empty cabbage field
gently rocking
an open blue umbrella, handle up

eating peanut brittle
on the great wall
it sticks to my teeth


summer, 1996 / sichuan, china

**night streets** in leshan
*march of the volunteers* (peoples' republic of china national anthem)


after dinner, would-be-bodhisattva goes for a walk
    *arise, ye who refuse to be slaves*
walking fathers wearing undershirts carry babies - toddlers running ahead
    *with our very flesh and blood*
vendors in rows of make-shift stalls sell cigarettes, bottled water, snack cakes
    *let us build our new great wall!*
noodles, shoes, kabobs, hot corn cobs, capitalism after hours
    *the peoples of china are in the most critical time*
old people, by the riverside, soar like cranes practicing qi gong
    *everybody must roar his defiance*
the streets and sidewalks filled
    *arise! arise! arise!*
would-be-bodhisattva and a nation walking just to be walking
    *millions of hearts with one mind*
this is night time in leshan
    *march on*
those who toil during the day at night are victorious
    *brave the enemy's gunfire*
spilling into and claiming the streets to do as they wish
    *brave the enemy's gunfire*
to sit on rough benches, play cards and smoke
    *march on*
7 young men watching while one fixes his motorcycle
    *march on*
    *march on, and on!*


summer, 1996 / sichuan, china

## the poverty of poverty

would-be-bodhisattva
doesn't know the language
is too shy to offer
to carry the double yoke basket
for an old woman who is
stepping slowly down the
slick cobble-stoned
back street
with her heavy load of plums

> would-be-bodhisattva
> has no workable plan
> to alleviate
> this suffering
> this endless toil

would-be-bodhisattva
thinks he is doing something
constructive by
letting the woman selling bananas
overcharge him
would-be-bodhisattva
then goes one mighty step further
and also lets her keep the change

summer, 1996 / sichuan, china

# japan snapshots

### on the plane

shoreline of snow wrinkled alaska
sunset
three fishing boats plow the waves home

two japanese businessmen
two tigers curled in sleep
two empty *saké* bottles

awake they ignored each other
now the american and japanese seatmates
face each other - in brotherly sleep

the rose-lipped japanese stewardess
each traveler forgets for a moment
they are lost

when the stewardess leaves
loneliness returns
more salty sweet peanuts

### first day

two young women giggle and turn away
from the elevator - too risky
to ride down with a bearded american

young woman office worker
in too much of a hurry
to tell me the name of this tranquil river

having my picture taken
while striking the sacred temple bell
shame resonates deep within

tired in kobe - almost not minding
my hosts playing and replaying
billy joel's greatest hits

### countryside

the frogs at dusk louder, louder
isshiki receives the night
house lights blink on, one, then another

the stillness of tenon-ji temple
only our muddy shoes and
a gentle rain waiting outside

my fingers read the shapes - buddha faces on worn tombstones
they too lean
bowing to the gleaming moon

white and gray cranes in the rice paddy
some unmoving, some alighting
"another haiku" yuko says

### tokyo

12 million people
in this city
alone in this small box of a room

my head on a buckwheat pillow
my dreams
seven thousand miles away

on the breeze -
the bursting azaleas' song
to which the iris sway

### bullet train

with the sea due south
and mount fuji hidden due north
why these lost feelings?

pulling down the shade
keeping the glare off his laptop
he'll miss seeing mount fuji

i knew it was mount fuji
but asked the steward anyway
to share my excitement with someone

### kyoto

fishing for haiku
at the taizo-in pond
too early for wisteria

wearing prayer beads as if holy
and the priest's ceremonial necklace
no one in my room to fool

walking down the streets of kyoto
saying to myself
"i'm walking down the streets of kyoto"

at nison-in temple - over the sound
of sacred crows
the clear temple bell of nearby jojakko-ji

powerful wings - mountain crows
beating the hot air
this summer afternoon

fighting or mating - two crows
dive from the roof of a nameless temple
at sunset

i am caught fully
by the summer – under this cherry tree
by the katsura

ignorant, i settle for information
from the guidebook
and from the squawkings of two nearby ducks

the sun has melted away
into evening clouds
6 businessmen - each with an ice cream cone

exotic kyoto
morning zazen in ancient myoshin-ji temple
nothing happens


may-june, 1999 / japan

cuckoo's cry

light rain in kyoto

    drips from the gingko trees and eaves

deepening my desire for you – my queen

    this evening

i imagine the arrangement

    and tangling - of our limbs

the cuckoo's cry is sharp

    then fades

        across the rooftops

may-june, 1999 / kyoto